Modern Rhymes DISCARDED About Ancient Times

ANCIENT AFRICA

Written by Susan Altman and Susan Lechner

Illustrated by Donna Perrone

Children's Press®
A Division of Scholastic Inc.
New York • Toronto • London • Auckland • Sydney
Mexico City • New Delhi • Hong Kong
Danbury, Connecticut

AND WHERE HUMAN LIFE BEGAN,

Raging rivers, desert sand.

Swamps and mountains, jungle green,

Animals not elsewhere seen.

Warriors with spear and shield,

Mysteries to be revealed.

Fabled kingdoms, jewels and gold,

Stories still not fully told.

Long-lost cities, Timbuktu,

All are waiting here for you.

Kings and queens from ancient times,

Learn about them from these rhymes.

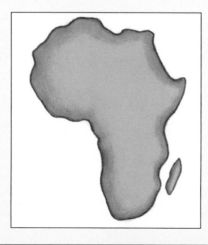

To C.J. and Kyle, for whom the promise of Africa is matched by their own great promise.—S.R.A.

To Devorah Scott—who has a heart as big as a continent.—S. L.

Reading Consultant: Nanci Vargus, Ed.D., Decatur Township Schools, Indianapolis, Indiana

Book production by Editorial Directions, Inc.

Book design by Marie O'Neill

Library of Congress Cataloging-in-Publication Data
Altman, Susan.
   Ancient Africa / written by Susan Altman and Susan Lechner ; illustrated by Donna Perrone.
      p. cm. — (Modern rhymes about ancient times)
   Includes bibliographical references (p.) and index.
   ISBN 0-516-21151-X (lib. bdg.) 0-516-27371-X (pbk.)
   1. Africa—Juvenile poetry. 2. History, Ancient—Juvenile poetry. 3. Children's poetry, American.
   [1. Africa—History—Poetry. 2. American poetry.]
   I. Lechner, Susan. II. Perrone, Donna, ill. III. Title.
   IV. Series.
   PS3551.L7943 A83 2001
   811'.54—dc21   2001028261

1 2 3 4 5 6 7 8 9 10 R 10 09 08 07 06 05 04 03 02 01

TABLE OF CONTENTS

NUBIA

To the south of Egypt's cloudless skies, the sun-scorched land of Nubia lay.

Ancient traders traveled its paths, their camels passing along the way.

The Nubian women were known for their grace, their elegant beauty, and pride.

Egyptian pharaohs would often choose a Nubian queen for a bride.

South of Egypt's cloudless skies stretched Nubia's sun-scorched land.

The kingdoms of Axum, Kerma, and Kush arose from its desert sand.

Though little is known of Nubia's ways, its mysteries beckon us still.

Historical treasure, a time beyond measure, its promises yet to fulfill.

Nubia is pronounced NEW-bee-uh. *Axum* is pronounced AK-sum. *Kush* is pronounced koosh.

KERMA

In a kingdom called Kerma,
The folks were well known
For making fine pots
That glittered and shone.

The merchants all gathered
In Kerma to trade.
And craftsmen would offer
The things they had made:

The kingdom of Kerma
Was something to see,
This realm south of Egypt—
2000 B.C.

In the 1920s, in the village of Nok,

Historians rolled their eyes in shock.

They found clay sculptures made from earth,

Years before the Christ child's birth.

Museums have them on display

So we can see this art today.

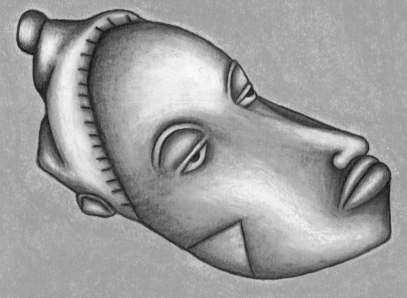

These sculptures were made between 900 B.C. and A.D. 200. The word *Nok* refers to the ancient people, the sculptures, and the village where they were found.

KUSH (750 B.C.–A.D. 300)

It's mentioned in the Bible—
This great and ancient land.
A kingdom known to all as Kush—
Famous, rich, and grand.

One thousand years Kush lasted,
Then all was swept away
By a kingdom known as Axum,
Which then began its sway.

Kush is pronounced koosh.

EROE, CAPITAL OF THE KUSH EMPIRE

This fabled ancient city
Was famous, rich, and pretty,
The capital and hub of mighty Kush.
It processed its iron ore
For use in peace and war,
Giving African technology a push.

This fabled ancient city
Was famous, rich, and pretty,
With pyramids and palaces aglow.
A meeting point for caravans
Traveling desert sands
To Meroe, a city on the go.

This fabled ancient city,
In Africa, so pretty,
Changed life across the land for all to see.
Iron weapons, tools, and rings,
And many other things,
Now had a solid-iron guarantee.

Meroe is pronounced MER-oh-ee.

AXUM (A.D. 300–A.D. 700)

It's said that ancient Axum
Was quite a lovely place.
The men were strong and handsome;
The women full of grace.
Its Red Sea docks and harbors
Brought merchants to its shore.
They came to buy rhinoceros horn,
Ivory, gems, and more.

The ancient king of Axum
Rode chariots of gold,
Pulled by four huge elephants,
And awesome to behold.
The Axum people minted coins,
Raised goats, and herded cattle.
Their armies fought with courage
And were greatly feared in battle.

Then soldiers led by Judith
Of the Agaw tribal band
Destroyed the Axum kingdom
And swept it from the land.

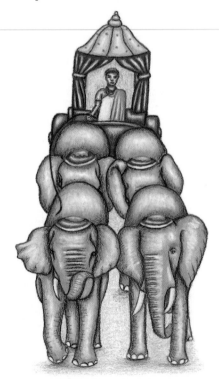

Axum is pronounced AK-sum.

12

KING EZANA (A.D. 300)

Ezana, king of Axum,
Protected caravans,
Defeated Kush and ruled supreme
According to his plans.

Ezana, king of Axum,
Became a Christian man.
He spread his new religion
To all those in his clan.

As Axum's state religion,
Christianity
Changed life for all the people
And Axum's history.

Ezana is pronounced ee-ZAH-nuh.

KINGDOM OF GHANA (Fourth century–1240)

In Egypt and Arabia,
From Cairo to Bombay,
The traders spoke of Ghana,
A kingdom far away.

It lay in western Africa.
Rich, respected, strong,
Its army feared by everyone
Who'd do a person wrong.

Known for gold and precious stones,
Textiles, salt, and honey,
Folks in Ghana had their fun,
Making lots of money.

Ghana is pronounced GAH-nuh.

# MALI KINGDOM (1235–late 1300s)

Between two tusks of ivory
Upon a throne of ebony,
The king of Mali ruled the land,
Maintaining peace and harmony.

Mali cities were renowned
For schools and scholarship.
Boys memorized Islamic thought
Without a single slip.

Its trade in copper, gold, and salt
Caused merchants to exclaim!
And kings like Mansa Musa
Brought Mali worldwide fame.

Mansa Musa is pronounced MAN-suh MOO-suh.
Mali is pronounced MA-le.

SUNDIATA KEITA (?–1255)

His name meant "Hungry Lion,"
And he gobbled up the land.
Established mighty Mali,
A kingdom proud and grand.

And though he had a painful limp,
He triumphed over foes,
This famous dark-skinned warrior,
And still his legend grows.

ANSA MUSA (?–1337)

Mansa Musa, Mansa Musa, a mighty Mali king.

The richest man in Africa, he owned 'most everything.

He took a trip to Mecca, where he told of Mali's fame,

And gave the people so much gold that all soon knew his name.

He spread the Mali Kingdom from the Niger to the sea

There was no crime; it was a time of great tranquility.

Mansa Musa, Mansa Musa, mighty Mali's pride.

Because of him, the Mali Kingdom

Soon was known worldwide.

Mansa Musa is pronounced
MAN-suh MOO-suh.

19

KENTE CLOTH/MUD CLOTH

Kente cloth is brightly colored—yellows, reds, and greens.

Woven first in Ghana, it was made for kings and queens.

The Kente name means "basket" for its lovely weavelike style.

And no matter where you wear it, it will always make you smile.

Now Mud cloth comes from Mali, and it's black, brown, yellow, white.

With geometric patterns it is worn both day or night.

The people soak the cloth in mud, then bleach out the design.

You'd think it would be yucky, but surprise! It looks just fine!

Kente is pronounced KEN-tay.

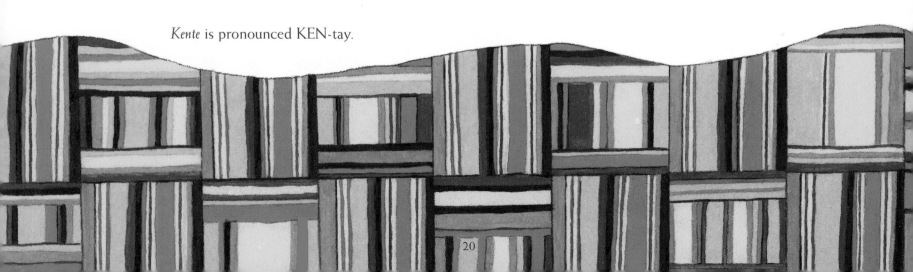

KOLA NUTS

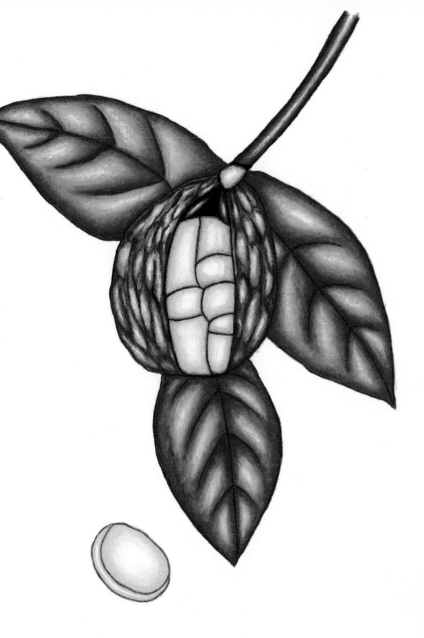

Kola nuts grow on a kola tree.
Africans eat them happily.
They're part of a special recipe
For soft drinks loved by you and me.

Kola nuts have earned great fame.
Can you guess what they became?
Here's a clue to make it plain.
It's half of Coca-Cola®'s name.

PYGMIES

Pygmy people are quite short.
They're less than five feet tall.
They hunt with poisoned arrows.
(They don't play basketball.)

Their clothes are made from pounded bark.
They like to dance and sing.
They know the ways of animals,
Can mimic anything.

They fade into the forest
When they want to disappear.
They move around so quietly
That no one else can hear.

IFE (Founded about A.D. 1300)

The kingdom of old Ife
Was noted for its art.
Fine carvings made of bronze and brass
Played a major part.

The kingdom now has disappeared,
The artworks still survive.
You find them in Nigeria.
It's history come alive.

Ife is pronounced EE-fay.

 IMBUKTU

Fabled city
Timbuktu,
Dusty traders' rendezvous.

Built by Tuareg
Long ago,
Reflected in historic glow.

Timbuktu is pronounced tim-buck-TOO.
Tuareg is pronounced TWA-reg.
Rendezvous (RON-day-vu) is
   the French word meaning "meeting."

The Tuareg were a dangerous tribal
group who lived in the desert and robbed
caravans that refused to pay them tribute.
Their descendants still live in the Sahara.

26

NDIAN OCEAN TRADE

Tortoiseshell and ivory,
Frankincense and glass,
Iron, gold, and ebony,
Sandalwood and brass.
All these things and many more
Formed a long-time trade.
On Africa's far eastern coast,
Vast fortunes could be made.
Fearless captains sailed their ships
Filled with goods to sell,
As far away as China—
An eager clientele.

From Zanzibar and Kilwa,
And towns in Mozambique,
Merchant seamen hoisted sail
Each day, week after week.
But soldiers came from Portugal,
Armed with gun and blade,
They burned these cities to the ground,
Destroying all the trade.

This trade took place between the tenth and fifteenth centuries.
These Portuguese attacks took place in the early 1500s.

MAASAI

Wish I could be a warrior
Just like the great Maasai,
Who made opponents tremble
Whenever they walked by.

To join the ranks of warrior,
A boy must show no fear.
His first test—kill a lion,
Alone, with just a spear.

They chased the slavers off their land,
Protected all their folk.
Their enemies soon learned Maasai
Were deadly to provoke.

Wish I could be a warrior
Just like the great Maasai.
Someday I'll go to Kenya,
Where I'll meet one and say, "Hi!"

Maasai is pronounce mah-SYE.

DOGON TRIBE

Their houses have sharp, pointed roofs.
The outside walls are round.
They're known for carving doors and masks,
The finest work around.

They're fond of things that come in twos.
Twins have a special place.
They watch the planets and the stars,
So far away in space.

They live in western Africa,
By River Niger's flow.
There, Dogon people live their lives
As they did long ago.

Dogon is pronounced DOH-gahn.

!KUNG SAN

To speak with a click
Is a difficult trick,
But the !Kung San folk do it quite well.
An African tribe
That's known far and wide
In the bright, sunny land where they dwell.

They live in the desert,
The great Kalahari,
(Not many enjoy living there)
With scorpions and snakes
That can cause awful aches.
(When you walk, you must
　　really take care.)

Instead of four seasons,
The !Kung San have six.
It works out quite well, I've been told.
They like to do dances,
Then fall into trances,
An interesting sight to behold!

To speak with a click
(A most difficult trick),
Touch the roof of your mouth with
　　your tongue.
You don't have to squeak—
Just "click" as you speak,
And you'll soon see just how it is done!

When a word is spelled with an exclamation point in front of it, it is spoken with a "click."
Kalahari is pronounced kal-uh-HAR-ee.

REAT ZIMBABWE (Built between 1200 and 1450)

Curving walls of massive stone
Standing silent, stern, alone.
The Shona built them long ago.
And that is almost all we know.

Zimbabwe is pronounced zim-BOB-whey.

# MONOMOTAPA KINGDOM (1440–1600s)

In what is now Zimbabwe, a kingdom once arose,

So rich its people often wore gold nuggets on their toes.

Its princes walked on golden floors 'mid lavish tapestries.

Ambassadors from foreign lands approached them on their knees.

But then came a rebellion, and the kingdom split in two.

It disappeared forever. Its glory days were through.

Monomotapa is pronounced MWAH-nah-moo-TOP-uh.

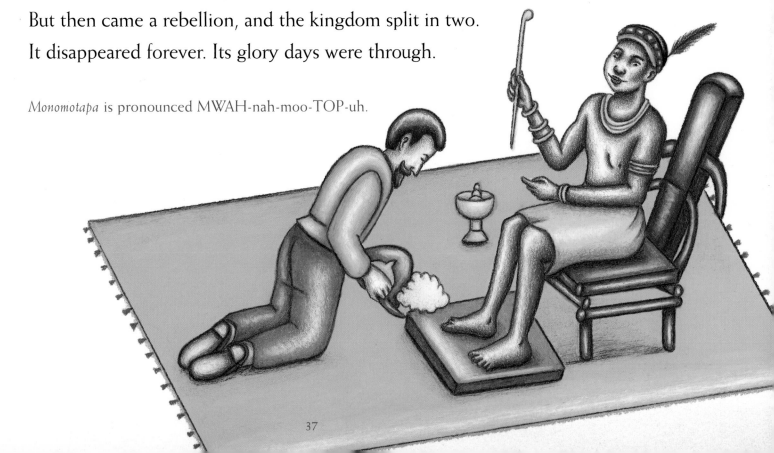

OORS

Sweeping out of Africa,
Conquerors of Spain,
Dark-skinned Muslim warriors
Rode to lasting fame.

They built great cities, aqueducts,
Universities,
Reservoirs and public baths,
Mosques and libraries.

They cultivated rice and silk,
Cotton, sugarcane.
Manufactured swords and shields,
Winning them great acclaim.

Sweeping out of Africa,
Conquerors of Spain,
Dark Islamic warriors
Set the world aflame.

TARIQ

An African named Tariq led his army into Spain,
Drove away the Spanish king
For an Islamic reign.

As general, he led his men with banners bright unfurled.
Tariq and his Moorish troops
Transformed the Spanish world.

Tariq is pronounced TAR-ick. The place where Tariq crossed from Africa into Spain was given the Arabic name *Jabal-al-Tariq*, which means "Tariq's mountain." Today that town and port is called Gibraltar.

LEO AFRICANUS (1485–1554)

Leo Africanus traveled all across the land,

Through mountains, over rivers, and across the desert sand.

Captured once by pirates, he later met the pope,

Who talked with him and told the world

That Leo was no dope.

He wrote a book on all he'd seen and opened people's eyes.

Too bad that he was born before they gave a Nobel prize!

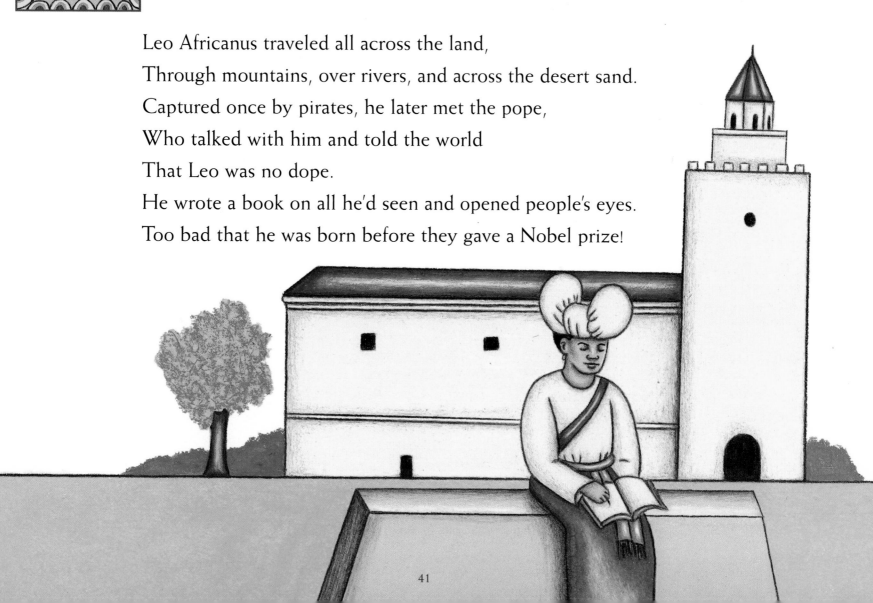

QUEEN NZINGA (1582–1663)

Nzinga, queen in Africa,
Won everlasting fame.
She had a mountain kingdom—
Matamba was its name.

And with her women warriors
She fought the Portuguese.
They hoped to drive her from her throne
And bring her to her knees.

They offered 'Zinga bags of gold.
They threatened her with a gun.
But they couldn't buy her off,
And they couldn't make her run.

They wanted slaves to sell abroad.
She said, "IT WILL NOT BE!"
Her soldiers fought war after war
To keep her people free.

Nzinga ruled for many years,
And when she died they missed her.
Nzinga, queen in Africa,
A proud, tough-minded sister!

Nzinga is pronounced en-ZING-gah. *Matamba* is pronounced mah-TOM-bah.

SHAKA (1787–1828)

Shaka, mighty Shaka, caused great fear and trepidation.

He conquered all his enemies and formed the Zulu Nation.

A strict disciplinarian—resourceful, brave and cruel—

He killed all who opposed him, and the rest bowed to his rule.

He's famous for his battle plans. He made weapons too.

And all the people trembled at what Shaka then might do.

His tactics still inspire those who lead troops into war.

His genius is a lasting part of military lore.

MORE ABOUT ANCIENT AFRICA

Books

Altman, Susan. *The Encyclopedia of African-American Heritage.* New York: Facts on File, 2000.

Haskins, Jim, and Kathleen Benson. *African Beginnings.* New York: Lothrop, Lee & Shepard, 1998.

Service, Pamela F. *The Ancient African Kingdom of Kush.* New York: Marshall Cavendish, 1998.

Sheehan, Sean. *Great African Kingdoms.* Austin, Tex.: Raintree/Steck-Vaughn, 1999.

WEBSITES

African Odyssey Interactive: History and Geography
http://artsedge.kennedy-center.org/aoi/resources/hg.html
Learn about Africa's ancient history on this website from the Kennedy Center

The Nok Museum
http://www.nokmuseum.org/index.html
Check out this virtual museum dedicated to African arts

Odyssey Online: Africa
http://www.emory.edu/CARLOS/ODYSSEY/AFRICA/ahomepg.html
Learn about ancient Africa from this website, sponsored by Emory University and the University of Rochester

Wonders of the African World
http://www.pbs.org/wonders/
Explore the lost wonders of ancient Africa on this PBS website

INDEX

ABOUT THE AUTHORS

Susan Altman and **Susan Lechner**, both graduates of Wellesley College, currently produce the Emmy Award–winning television program *It's Academic* in Washington, D.C., and Baltimore, Maryland. They have also produced *It's Elementary*, *Heads Up!*, and *Pick Up the Beat*. They are co authors of *Followers of the North Star*, a book of rhymes for young people (also published by Children's Press). Ms. Altman is also the author of the play *Out of the Whirlwind* and the books *Extraordinary African-Americans*, and *The Encyclopedia of African-American Heritage*.